# THE BEST VIEW ON THE FARM

*Looking at the Minnesota River Valley*

## JOHN HOMME

Printed by Lightning Source
1246 Heil Quaker Blvd. La Vergne, TN USA 37086
ISBN – 978-1-0878-8018-1
Unless otherwise noted, Scripture quotations are from The Holy Bible, New International Version®, NIV®. Copyright © 1973, 1978, 1984, 2011 by Biblica, Inc.™ Used by permission of Zondervan.

Cover Design by Daniel Ojedokun
Interior Design by Pyramid Publishers
Printed in the United States of America

# Contents

*But the basic reality of God is plain enough. Open your eyes and there it is! By taking a long and thoughtful look at what God has created, people have always been able to see what their eyes as such can't see: eternal power, for instance, and the mystery of his divine being. So nobody has a good excuse.* Romans 1:19-20  The Message

# Forward

This photo captures the beauty of the Minnesota River Valley. My vantage point is about 200 feet above the river level. I am looking at a bend in the river that we have always referred to as The High Bank. It is the God-given beauty of this farm that has kept my attention for 70 plus years. Many others have visited and shared my feelings about this special place. The farm location is six miles south of Sacred Heart, Minnesota. In this book I share the history of this farm, my history on it, and many stories that illustrate my connections to it.

In the words of my good friend Dave Rodquist:

The mystic call of the rural Minnesota River Valley is like none other. It calls to all who have a heart for a simpler life . . . if only for a few hours or a mere day or two . . . to pause, and experience the wonders of our Creator. Maybe it's the kaleidoscope of colors as starry nights welcome warm sunny days; or the slap of a beaver's tail at rivers edge; or the sight and sound of Canadian honkers flying low in a misty fall morning; or the quiet creep of a white-tail deer at the break of dawn; or a gobbler's response, to a first-time hunter's call. Whatever it is, it's unforgettable . . . especially when shared with a good friend or two, in the mysterious wonder of the rural Minnesota River Valley.

# Chapter 1

# At the Beginning

Late September was still warm as the Minnesota Volunteers under the command of Henry Sibley set up camp on the shores of Battle Lake. They were about four miles south of Upper Sioux Agency Minnesota. The day was September 22, 1862, and Sibley knew that the Dakota warriors were near. He set up perimeter patrols and the men bedded down for the evening. That night a large group of Dakota men led by Ta Oyate Duta assembled near Sibley's men, taking cover in tall grass. The plan was to ambush Sibley's men in the morning as they broke camp. The following morning some of Sibley's men, on route to get more food, surprised the concealed Dakota men who fired shots. That aroused Sibley's camp to the location of the Dakota. Within two hours the outnumbered defeated Dakota fled into the surrounding countryside. The Great Sioux Uprising of 1862 was over.

Here is a first-hand account of the Battle of Wood Lake given by Wamditanka (Jerome Big Eagle), a Dakota who led fighters into battle against Sibley's troops. In his words:

"We expected to throw the whole white force into confusion by [a] sudden and unexpected attack, Wamditanka later recalled. I think this was a good plan of battle. Our concealed men would not have been discovered. The grass was tall and the place by the road and the ravine were good hiding places. . . . The morning came and an accident spoiled our plans. For some reason, Sibley did not move early, as we expected. It seemed a considerable time after sun-up when four or five wagons with some soldiers started from the camp in the direction of the old Yellow Medicine Agency . . . They came on over the prairie, right where part of our line was. Some of the wagons were not on the road, and if they had kept straight on would have driven right over where our men were as they lay in the grass. At last, they came so close that our men had to rise and fire. This brought on the fight of course, but not according to the way we had planned it. Little Crow saw it and felt very badly."

Before 1862, the Sioux (Dakota) owned 10 miles on either side of the Minnesota River where they hunted and fished to feed their families. Some settlers lived for the most part within the Indian property boundary. One of these was Joseph R. Brown and his wife, Susan, who was part Indian; he built a granite veneer home about three miles downriver from our family farm. Brown had a varied background, including being a U.S. Indian Agent until 1861. The home's granite walls were a defense against any attacks, but the cedar shingles were a weak design point. While he was away on business in 1862, Dakota warriors burned down his house and took his family captive. They were later released.

After the war, the government placed the Dakota on two reservations: the Upper Sioux Agency, located four miles north of the final battle of the war, and the Lower Sioux Agency. The government took possession of the prime land that was then divided and sold. Since most of the land was tallgrass prairie, they added a wood lot to each parcel sold to provide logs for building houses and firewood to heat them. The wood lots were located near the river.

It was into this area in the spring of 1867 that my great grandfather Ole Gjermundson Homme brought his family from Satersdal, Norway. Relatives informed him that a tract of land 1 ½ miles south of the Upper Sioux Agency was for sale. When he saw it, he exclaimed, "Here I want to live, and here I want to die." He paid $1.25 per acre for the land that is now the Homme homestead. An unverified family story is that Ole borrowed money from his brother to buy the land. His brother Jim had gone to California in 1849 and found a significant amount of gold.

Twenty miles downriver in the Minnesota River Valley was Ole Olson Enestvedt and Anne Kittilsland's farm. It was there that my maternal grandfather, Theodore Enestvedt, was born June 14, 1875. Theodore married my grandmother Lena in 1903. All my ancestors had two things in common: first, they came from Norway and second, they lived within 10 miles of the Minnesota River.

Downriver five miles, the Peder Kollen family bought land on both sides of the Minnesota River in 1871. On the south side of the Minnesota River was the homestead with some farmland. It was located on granite deposits that surfaced and went underground all along the river. On the north side of the river across from the Kollens, they owned a farm of 240-acre farm as well. My paternal grandmother, Jergina Kollen, married my grandfather Knute Homme. One of her sisters, Sarah, was the owner of the farm on the north side of the river. My father Peter and my mother Lena married in the late 1930s and lived in a log home built in the 1860s on Sarah's farm. On the bank of the Meadow Creek, on the far side of the culvert, is a depression in the hillside. Word is that the family that built the log home on our farm lived the first winter there. A depression cut into the hillside, called a dugout, had a log roof, sides, and front. Meadow Creek provided water as it remained melted through the winter.

My father farmed on shares for his Aunt Sarah until she died in 1968; then he bought the farm from her estate. One of our pre-winter jobs was to cut and split firewood for Aunt Sarah and her sister, Aunt Petra. We had an old David Bradley (Sears) chainsaw to cut down trees plus a tractor-mounted cutoff saw to cut logs to length. Then we hand split the ash. When we had a truckload (a ton and a half), we took it to Sarah's and stacked it in her shed that was cut into a large granite boulder. It was cool in the summer and was used for storing vegetables.

After my mother, Lena, graduated from high school, she took a short teacher preparation course. She taught in a one-room schoolhouse in the river valley. She had to get there early to start the stove. When her three children were old enough, she went to college for more training and became a reading teacher until she retired in her 60's.

Her favorite retirement activity was quilting—making master-pieces for her children and grandchildren. She made a graduation quilt for our son Jim called "Barns in the Family" that had scenes of nine barns from the Homme, Enestvedt, and Williams families. She entered it in the Minnesota State Fair and won a first-place ribbon. She achieved the status of a Master Quilter and mentored many young quilters.

Our farm bordered the Minnesota River. We lived in the log home that had no running water or indoor plumbing until 1948. The logs had been covered with steel siding to protect them from the elements. We then moved to Sacred Heart, Minnesota, located six miles north of the farm. Father drove to the farm each day and called himself a "suitcase farmer." While we lived on the farm we had milk cows and chickens as well as raised crops. After moving, we raised corn & soybeans, with some small grain added in for crop rotation. The Minnesota River affected our lives the 70 plus years of my life. It gives me a great sense of pride that my great grandfather acquired the land from the government, passed it down to my grandfather, who passed it down to my father, and it finally came to my siblings and me. I now own this land next to the river that has such a rich family history, and I will pass it on to my children.

# Chapter 2

# Before the Beginning

The Minnesota River Valley is up to five miles wide and up to 250 feet deep. Water does not get close to filling that volume so where did that size come from? At the end of the last glacial period, the meltwater formed a very large glacial lake in central North America called Lake Agassiz. At its largest, Lake Agassiz was larger than the combined area of the Great Lakes. As melting ice filled it and the ice on Hudson's Bay melted, Lake Agassiz flowed north in what is now the Red River Basin. The Glacial River Warren flowed south from Lake Agassiz carving out the Minnesota River Valley. The Minnesota River flows southeast to present-day Mankato. It then turns northeast to the present-day Twin Cities where it joins the Mississippi River. On average, the River Warren flow was about 100 times that of the present-day Minnesota River.

The Glacial River Warren cut through layers of glacial sediments of clay, silt, sand, gravel, and boulders. In some places it cut down to some of the oldest bedrock in North America known as Morton Gneiss. This rock, called granite, appears at various places in the valley such as Granite Falls, south of Sacred Heart and Morton. Between those locations, it dives underground to reappear at another downriver location. At the Kollen farm is a bowl-shaped hole on top of one of the large granite outcrops. It was cut by a rock spun by river current over a long period. Near our farm are several granite quarries. They have large derricks that lift the cut stone out to make into building stone for monuments and structures. Local businesses make grave markers and other monument markers. Many of the quarries are no longer active but filled with rainwater. As an adolescent, I spent many hours swimming in these pools.

One, in particular, was close to the road from my work site, and I would often stop with a bar of soap after work for a refreshing dip. Some of the crushed stone forms road base. On one of our river trips, I pointed out grooves on granite and told my sons that they were from glaciers moving over the rocks.

The receding River Warren deposited large amounts of sand, gravel, and clay. These deposits can be used for road building, railroad base, and construction. Our farm has such deposits, though we haven't developed them commercially. A neighbor has a large deposit of white kaolin clay used for printing, cement, bricks, and ceramics.

After time, the Minnesota River settled into the River Warren basin. Erosion processes worked as lands drained within the watershed to the river. These forces formed gullies or ravines as we call them. As these ravines grew in size, different trees, plants and animals are found there. Oak, ash, basswood, cedar, and ironwood grew in these ravines. Next to the river were maple, basswood, cottonwood, and other water-tolerant species.

# Chapter 3

# After the Beginning

Since my ancestors settled by or near the Minnesota River, the stream has changed. Some changes were subtle and some were not. The river itself is 370 miles long, emptying into the Mississippi at St. Paul. Its watershed drains about 1/5$^{th}$ of the state, 17,000 square miles in the southern and western part. The following rivers form its watershed—the Le Sueur, Cottonwood, Watonwan, Redwood, Hawk Creek, Blue Earth, Yellow Medicine, Pomme de Terre, Sand Hill, Chippewa, Credit, Little Cottonwood, Whetstone, Little Minnesota, Rush, Crow, Rock, and Bois de Sioux. The watershed and the rivers are dynamic systems subject to God given natural forces and man-made activities.

Each of the rivers (watersheds) that empty into the Minnesota River bring their own additions to the main body of water. The Minnesota is a muddy river because the land that it drains adds silt to it. Throughout its meandering path, it cuts land from outside curves and replaces it on inside curves. The meandering often put boundaries that were once on dry land in the middle of the stream. This often makes it difficult to identify the boundaries.

Most changes over the past 150 years are as a result of human activities. These activities include home building, road building, farming, tiling, herbicide use, logging, recreational activities, hunting, and fishing. These activities have affected the river valley. Yet its natural beauty and vibrance still influence those who experience it.

# Chapter 4

# Farmland, Woodlots, and Suitcase Farming

When the government took control of the previous Dakota land after 1862, it was decided that it would be sold for farmland. Land outside the Minnesota River Valley was tallgrass prairie that was refreshed by naturally occurring fires. Buffalo roamed the land; their numbers were extraordinary. Farmers plowed and planted the land that controlled the grass fires as well, but there were very few trees on the prairie. For this reason, the government deeded a wood lot with each farmland parcel sold. These woodlots were generally within the floodplain of the Minnesota River and supplied wood for building and firewood. As these woodlots became less important to prairie farmers, my father started to accumulate them. At one point we owned about 25 acres of woodlots. One, in particular, we call "the 5-acre piece" because it was five acres of land in the middle of the forest that had been cleared by one man, Westly Benish. Westly was a laborer who lived a mile upstream from our farm in a modest home. He cleared the 5-acre piece with an ax and kept some cows there for grazing. He worked for my father at various times helping on the farm. He lived off the river using set lines to catch catfish that were very good eating. He once brought us a huge catfish whose head covered the whole bottom of a garbage can. He sold the 5-acre piece to my father, and we farmed it for many years. Because of the tall trees on both sides of the narrow piece, a lack of sunlight didn't produce as good a crop yield as the rest of the farm.

Being "suitcase" farmers had its set of challenges, one of which was moving machinery from the river farm to The Howell Place that was six miles south. To do so required crossing the river some-times with equipment that had inches to spare on each side of the bridge. A new bridge made the crossing easier. Moving machinery usually took two people, one to drive the equipment and one to pick up the other person at the other end. My father solved this issue by buying a small Honda motorbike that he strapped to the side of the tractor for his return trip.

One of Dad's favorite winter forms of exercise was to cut trees that shaded the crops from the edge of the fields. My brother Tru-man and I got much exercise and chain saw experience on these outings. Most trees were box elder and had no commercial value.

Another issue of not living on the farm was protecting things from being stolen. Gasoline was the favorite target. To protect the tank, the first defense was a padlock for the nozzle that helped but could be bypassed with a bolt cutter. We then moved the tank inside the machine shed, but a thief found his way in through the back door. We were stymied until a neighbor driving by spotted a white 1950 Ford sitting behind the shed. We then fortified the back door and put up a small sign targeting a neighbor youth say-ing, "Art, how would you like to make twine in Stillwater?" It was reported that Art soon left for another place to live. Uncle Ole had another solution to gas thieves, which was to place a half stick of dynamite high in a tree above the gas tank. He wired the charge to the nozzle and a neighbor reported hearing a loud noise one night.

The farmland in the river valley had its own microclimate that produced different crop yields; some crop varieties did better. My father and Uncle Kenneth were both Certified and Registered Seed Growers. Those designations meant that they had good farming practices and could sell seed varieties with those labels on them. There were only 100 Registered Seed Growers in the state, and they received new varieties of seeds developed by the University of Minnesota, a Land Grant university. Dad and Uncle Kenneth would plant the new varieties, harvest them, clean them, and sell the seed to local farmers. Part of doing that process was to analyze or certify the quality of the seed.

One of the tests was germination, which means what percent

of the seed could be expected to produce a root and grow into a plant when put in the ground. To measure germination, we would wrap 20 seeds in a damp sock inside a jar and put the jar behind the stove for several days. The jar was then opened and the number of seeds that produced a root were counted and the germination rate was established. Usually, we expected it to be over 90%.

A bag tag is another item that was prepared for the sale of seeds that included the variety name, farmer, year of growth, and germination rate. We had a small spirit duplicator for preparing the tags. During the spring we would take the seed from the bin, run it through a fanning mill to clean it, and put it into two-bushel bags that weighed 120 pounds. I developed very strong hands and arms from handling these bags and was happy when Dad switched to 90-pound bags.

There was also a two-story granary on the farm near the road, with a sloped access that allowed us to put grain in the upper story with ease. From the upper story, the grain could be put into bins in the lower story. Often the transfer of grain took place as the grain was cleaned by running it through a fanning mill. The fanning mill consisted of a hopper to control flow through a series of sieves. Some of the sieves were larger than the grain and separated any larger pieces of trash. Next were smaller sieves that separated our smaller items. The last part of the process was to drop the grain past a four-bladed fan that separated items that were lighter than the grain. Cleaned grain was then stored in a lower-level bin or put directly into bags. The mill was powered by a small gasoline motor.

The interior walls of the granary were rough sawed lumber and the outside was covered by corrugated metal. Its roof, like that of the barn, also failed; and one February day we decided to burn it down and bury the remains. Used oil was the fire staring agent. The fire started slowly and when it went through the roof the flames became very hot and tall. When it burned through the met-al walls, we could feel that the temperature might have jumped 500 degrees. It was so hot that we had to move cars that were parked on the county road. The day was very windy, fanning the flames and blew them far enough to burn the top of an oak tree about

100 yards downwind. It was quite a sight to watch, and within 45 minutes there were just some smoldering coals on the ground. I now regret that I did not salvage some of the interior wood that was white oak and ash that would have made some great wood to build things with.

Our cousins who lived about four miles down the river were corn breeders. They produced Enestvedt Minnhybrid Seed Corn (later changed to Enestvedt Seed Company). Hybrid corn was bred for the local area's climate and growing season. The Enestvedts used water from the river to irrigate their corn during dry spells.

To produce hybrid corn, the breeder would use a four-row corn planter that contained three rows of "mother" seed and the outside row of "father" seed. When the farmer turned around at the end of the field and came back he had made a pattern of two rows of "father" corn and six rows of "mother" corn. Corn normally pollinates itself to produce kernels by pollen dropping from the tassel at top of the plant to the silk that is in the middle of the plant. This combination produces kernels within the husk. Detasseling is done to the "mother" plants so that the pollen from the "father" rows pollinates the "mother" plants. This method of producing hybrid corn began in the mid-1930s, providing countless numbers of young people summer jobs detasseling at Enestvedt's. Hybrid corn seeds produce significantly higher yields because they have the combined desirable attributes of the "mother" and "father" varieties.

I didn't do any detasseling for the Enestvedts but ran detasseling crews for Dekalb under the supervision of my Uncle Jerry Peterson who was an area manager for that large seed company. At first, I supervised walking crews consisting of 30 youngsters and two supervisors. The taller kids finished their rows more quickly, and we had to convince them that it would be a good idea to go back and help the slower pickers. The following several years I ran machine crews that consisted of six girls with good skills. They rode on a machine with a single drive wheel in front and platforms for the girls to stand on while picking. I sat in the back, drove the machine, and sometimes fell asleep because the machine drove itself by the front wheel following the furrow between the cornrows. More than once the girls woke me up at the end of the row. After three years of machine work, I was moved to the role of inspector. For this role, I went to Dekalb, Illinois, to be trained and see the home office. Inspecting a field after it was de-tasseled involved walking into a random part of the field and start counting stalks with one counter and counting remaining tassels with another counter. The averaged tassel counts needed to be below 3 % to pass; otherwise a crew was sent through to remove more tassels.

During the summer after I graduated from high school, I contracted to cut down 200 trees on the western edge of the farm to make way for a new culvert over Meadow Creek . Most of the trees were less than six inches in diameter, but there were some nice-sized white oaks and a huge white elm that sat right at the edge of the creek. The white elm was about three feet across at the base and I had to do several undercuts to get it to fall. I cut the branches off, which left a huge log that I saved for future use. (I never found a use for it.) We kept some of the oak logs that were later sawed into lumber.

The contractor for the culvert was a local man who had hired my Uncle Lewis Enestvedt to run his bulldozer. Lewis had been from Alaska to Australia using his heavy equipment skills on various projects. He pushed the dead trees into several piles that we burned and cut an opening through where a 7-foot triangular culvert was to be placed. A friend, Paul Schwinghammer, and I were given the job of assembling the culvert. It took us several days of the assembly until its 40-foot long piece was ready to be put in place. The culvert serviced the creek for almost 60 years when a large rainfall washed it out. It was bent too much to repair so was replaced with a concrete culvert about 3 years ago.

My father, Peter Homme, retired from farming in 1973. As is typical in such events, there was a farm auction to liquidate unneeded equipment. I took a day off of teaching and went to help. There was a good turnout, and we had been warned ahead of time to prepare for some auction tricks. One of which was to disconnect a spark plug from any equipment with a motor, especially tractors.

The effect was that the tractor would not run well and sold for a price lower than its worth. Dad's best tractor was a 1963 John Deer Diesel 3010 that was in very good shape. Uncle Ole was at the sale and wanted me to bid for him because he didn't hear very well. The tractor bidding started briskly, and Ole won it paying more for the used tractor than dad paid for it 10 years earlier. Other items sold that day were a corn planter, corn picker, trailers, a 1937 Dodge 1 ½ ton truck, other tractors, plows, mowers, disks, corn sheller, cultivators, and other miscellaneous items as the sale bill announced. The sale was a grand day and a transition to retirement for Dad. Even in retirement, he went to the farm almost every day to keep track of the renter and usually walked up a 100-yard 30-degree slope to keep in shape.

When we built a new house in 1973, I took trees from the river valley for the yard. Next to the river, I found a 25-foot tall maple tree that was about 4 inches across at its base. It was tall and thin because it was reaching for sunlight through the forest canopy. Its length made transporting it a challenge, but I planted it about 20 feet off the southwest corner of the house. It didn't gain much height but is now 16 inchs wide at the base, with many branches that provide much shade to the deck under it. The farm provided two hackberry trees that provide good shade, a basswood that has beautiful fall colors, and my favorite tree—the Quaking Aspen. Its small round leaves shimmer when the wind hits them and also produce a distinctive sound. In the fall, the leaves turn yellow and are usually the last to fall. It is a delight of color, movement, and sound.

In 2002 my mother, Lena Homme, enrolled about 120 acres of the farm in the Minnesota Conservation Reserve Enhancement Program (CREP). As the landowner, she received the value of the land in payments from the state, spaced over 15 years. The land could not be farmed for cash crops, had to be planted in a cover crop such as tall prairie grass, and the weeds had to be controlled. The CREP program aim is to have the land transform into prairie grasses as it was before settlement. The landowner is required to do a mid-contract burn to help control weeds and to stimulate the grass to take over. Our first Big Burn in 2010 was to comply with the CREP mid-contract burn requirement, which was to stimulate the growth of the grasses, destroy weed seeds, and burn scrub trees. I went to a DNR class called "Learn to Burn" where I found out what wind, moisture, and containment conditions were required for a safe fire. I recruited about 15 people to help with the burn, some with ATVs and one with a water truck. The County Soil and Water folks provided fire swatters, water backpacks, and fire starter drip cans. The swatters were used to smother small fires, the water backpacks had spray nozzles to put out the fire, and the drip cans were supposed to drip fire on the grass to start it burning. We never did get the drip cans to work because the tops were on backward. With an east wind, things started pretty well because the river and a neighbor's field were adequate firestops on the west side of the grassland. A backpack and a couple of swatters that some of the crew forgot to remove from the downwind side of the fire were burned. That was a $150 lesson we learned. See Big Burn III Movie April 10, 2016. Two previous burns occurred in 2013 and 2010. https://youtu.be/p3Q3WpAMx14.

The landowner retains ownership, pays taxes, and controls weeds. There is a fairy tale about killing the goose that laid the golden egg, which pretty much describes our experience with the CREP program.

Because the farm produced no income after the CREP payments finished, I was always looking for income sources. The DNR offered a program to cut cedars off the hillsides because the cedar trees had prevented the native prairie grasses from growing. So an unemployed friend and I spent six days cutting cedar trees off five acres of hillside. When we finished, I noted that we had some large logs, one 24-inches wide. So I asked a neighbor if there was a sawmill close. He said there was one across the river about four miles away. It was there that I met Glenn Huseby, a true renaissance man who had many talents. These included saw milling, building, old building restoration, and woodworking. Glenn was not afraid to try just about anything. He had a Wood Mizer saw that was a band saw that moved down the log on rollers. The log was clamped on a rack that fit between the tracks that rollers ran on. Glenn asked me what I wanted to do with the cut cedar and I said, "Probably make cedar chests." He told me how to make the cedar chests and at this writing, I have made 20 of them for my granddaughters, nieces, nephews, and friends. Red cedar is a wood with beautiful pink, red, and white tones intermixed. It also has the characteristic of repelling wool-eating moths; red cedar chests were prized for their ability to keep heirlooms safe. I soon found that cutting the cedar in one-inch thicknesses was the best for making cedar chests. Glenn did much of the sawing for me, charging a reasonable hourly rate. After a while, he said, "You know how to do this; go ahead on your own." Even though he charged me a lower rate when I sawed, it often turned out better to pay him the higher rate because of his efficiency.

My granddaughter Emily made the first one with me that we filmed with the title, "Building a Cedar Chest." It is on YouTube and has over 100,000 views. See Building a Cedar Chest Movie August 25, 2009. https://www.youtube.com/watch?v=T6Z3ull3s-A shows how to "Build a Cedar Chest" from rough sawn cedar to finished product. Because of Emily's bubbly personality and camera presence, the video was well received. I have made many movies with my grandchildren, most of which are loosely scripted and make use of their personalities to tell a story. More about that later. Using cedar that was not of "chest quality" I also made about a dozen Adirondack chairs. These looked great when finished and covered with urethane but would weather to a dull grey outside.

After sawing a lot of cedar, we decided to build a house and thought it would be cool to use oak from the farm for flooring. Again, some friends helped me cut down white oak from the farm to make about 800 board feet of lumber. We took the oak to my friend Jim Raymond who had a large facility for cutting logs, kiln drying the wood, and a shaper for making tongue and groove flooring. After the oak had air-dried, Jim turned it into flooring for me. I used it in two additions that we added to our house. I also made a porch swing and other furniture from the oak and some ash logs that we sawed with Glenn's help. We also sawed some ash logs that are light-colored wood that I used for making a glider chair.

In the 1970s, Dutch Elm disease went through the river valley killing most of the elm trees. There were two varieties—white
elm and red elm. The white elm soon decayed, but the red elm
was much harder, and when the bark fell off it made excellent firewood that we used in our Plymouth home and still use today in the
Homme Hilton, more about the Hilton later. We also burn Ironwood that is very dense and burns like coal.

My father always encouraged me in whatever new thing I
tried. Whether hunting for wind generators in South Dakota or
buying me a new rototiller when I started gardening, he always
found a way to encourage me. When we started burning red elm
from the farm, he bought two chain saws and a wood splitter, making them available for my use. He also instilled trust in me. When
I started college, he took me to his bank and told the banker that I
would be signing his name to his checks for whatever I needed in
college. This went on until I finished college.

Invasive plant species and bugs have changed the ecosystem of
the river valley. Already-mentioned Dutch elm disease has killed
most of the native white and red elm. Common buckthorn has tak-
en over the edge of forested lands and crowded out native shrubs
like chokecherry and sumac. Garlic mustard is a plant that can
produce hundreds of tiny seeds for quick takeover. Dense patches of it can displace important native flowers, tree seedlings, and
grasses. Emerald ash borer is an invasive insect from Asia respon-
sible for the deaths of millions of ash trees. Ash borer is making its
way through the river valley.

Buckthorn control has been a constant issue at the farm since
its appearance in the early 2000s. At first, I tried to spray it with
Roundup, which had some effect. I then used a weed whip with
a saw blade attachment and then put a spray-on Roundup in the
stem again with some effect. I talked to the DNR about buckthorn
control funding. Over the winter, I talked to several guys that had
skid steer mounted devices to cut the buckthorn to the ground.
The plan was to follow the cutting up with a spray called Garlon-4
in the fall. I found Cody Nelson, who lives across the river, and

the rest is chronicled in "Cody and the Ambusher" https://youtu.be/kbXqqsI0wEc in which his Case TR 270 with the Ambusher attachment cut buckthorn on our farm. After 3 hours of cutting, we had a good amount of the buckthorn down. Later in the fall, I went back to see if there were any leaves on the plants indicating if they were alive. I found very few leaves.

In addition to trees for wood, some types produce fruits that we use for making jelly. Chokecherries ripen about the third week in July and make a tart jelly that I usually cut with some apple juice to make it milder. See Granddaughter Maggie in "How Chokecherries Got Their Name" https://youtu.be/PVx8G0JZBSY showing how chokecherries got their name and how to make chokecherry jelly. Maggie is very experienced in front of the camera and often does voiceovers (narrations) in my movies. We usually get adequate chokecherries to pick two of every three years.

Chokecherries are found in many places on the farm. One group of trees was next to the county road and Dad would park the 37 Dodge truck next to the trees. We would then pull the branches over the truck bed, sometimes using a rope to hold them and pick the chokecherries. Mom would then make them into jelly. Her recipe uses the berries juice full strength. My sister Marge uses mom's recipe. I have learned that preparing the jelly that way is a little too strong for most folks so I tone it down by adding some apple juice to my recipe.

Wild Grapes and wild plums ripen in early September. Usually, we mix those two to make a very nice combination of jelly. See granddaughters Savannah and Veronica in "A Grape Time Making Jelly (alsoPlum)" https://youtu.be/7vU9aIa4VcA that shows son Peter and kids picking and making wild grape and plum jelly. We usually get adequate grapes and plums to pick three of every four years. We use ½ pint jars of jelly as gifts and get many requests for more.

Grandmother Enestvedt had a large arbor of concord grapes that mom was allowed to use for making a very refreshing grape drink. She stored it in the cool basement and brought some out on hot summer days for a refreshing drink.

# Chapter 5

# Tiling

Up until the late 1940s and early '50s, many small lakes or sloughs existed in the Minnesota River Watershed. They provided much local habitat for small animals and birds as well as stopover areas for migrating ducks and geese. They slowly drained to the Minnesota and rains replenished their volumes. My cousin Burt Enestvedt once said, "There was usually one drainage culvert in a section of land and a skunk usually had that plugged with their nest." The effect of this cycle was to keep the level of the river stable so that boats could navigate as far upstream as Granite Falls. Mail boats made regular stops on the river until replaced by overland routes.

Post-World War II America's population grew and there was a need for more agricultural production. Higher yielding seed varieties and more land met that need. Drain tile was introduced into the watershed that emptied into natural drainage channels such as creeks and gullies. Soon drainage ditches were dug to speed and direct the water flow in the watershed. They were so successful that more drain tile was installed. Most sloughs and small lakes became new farmland.

There was a saying in my environmental education classes that, "Everything is connected to everything else; everything goes someplace and there is no such thing as a free lunch." This succinctly covers the story of drain tile and the Minnesota watershed. The everything connected water cycle of rain, runoff, evaporation, and rain powers the watershed. During that cycle, water drains someplace and the timing and volume of that drainage affects the watershed. On the plus side, desired drainage produces more tillable land. On the minus side of tiling is a loss of much water habitat, interruption of migration patterns, increased water flow periods, increased erosion, great fluctuations in river levels, and introduction of agricultural chemicals into the watershed. The building of highways, streets, and parking lots also increases the speed of drainage in the watershed. Current practice and drainage law work to control the negative effects of drainage but there is little one can do to reverse the process.

# Chapter 6

# Floods

Spring runoff of melting snow produces high water in the river. The amount of snow cover and how fast it melts determine how high the river will get and how long it stays that way. Small snowmelt might mean that the river stays within its banks, but about one in three years the river covers part of our lower field. About every ten years it might cover half of the lower field—about 70 acres. Up to the present day, if it receded in time, we could plant crops as usual but sometimes the ground was wet well into June. This caused late plantings (usually meaning soybeans) because they would mature and still produce a crop. I remember one time when we had a hail storm that did a lot of damage to our soybean field. We had crop insurance, but by the time the insurance adjuster got there, the field was underwater. The adjuster said, "I can't pay for damage I can't see," which upset my father. We got our insurance premium returned but no hail damage payments.

Uncle Ole and his son, Cousin Paul, farmed in the river valley about five miles downriver from Granite Falls. After one heavy rainstorm, the river level went up so quickly that it covered one of Paul's tractors underwater up to the exhaust pipe. He could see it but had no way of retrieving it until the water receded. When he could finally get to it, he drained all the oil, coolant, and cavities that held water. He put in fresh fluids and a new battery, and it started no worse for the experience.

In 2011, neighbor Andy Holt set a game camera recording three photos each day at 11 AM. It ran from the middle of March to the middle of June 2011. It showed the snow disappear, the river rise and fall, and the presence of a turkey and a deer. It also showed the temperature and pressure changes and the land green-up. See Farm Time Lapse, Jul 31, 2011, https://youtu.be/MvvH4JgcvSc

Meadow Creek runs on the northern border of our farm and goes on to the river through our neighbor's field. During one high water event in the creek, our neighbors decided to build a dam where it crossed their field. Meadow Creek changed its course to border the western part of the farm, cutting a deep channel on the edge of the field. At one time, my boys and I went bone hunting in the creek bed, which involved finding things that don't look like rocks. Sometimes it was a rock and sometimes it was a skull or a horn. While exploring the channel, we found two bucket loads of buffalo horns that we took to the University of Minnesota. They identified them as Bison.

During another flood, one of our neighbors, Lenny Holt, got his photo taken in a 10-foot-high deer stand in our field. The flood covered everything but the top foot; Lenny and his sons got there by boat.

Almost every biology or ecology class includes the story of how the Nile River in Egypt spring floods bring thick rich mud (black silt) that provides excellent soil to plant seeds. The ancient Egyptians would grow good crops in the mud left behind when the Nile flooded. That may be the case in that water system, but we have rarely observed beneficial things left behind when the Minnesota floods. There sometimes would be tree branches, various objects the stream had picked up, and weed seeds. The weed that my father worked hard to eradicate was wild artichoke, a large and hearty plant. He would get rid of it, and the next flood would replenish the population. Cocklebur is another less noxious weed that is easily killed in corn but has to be chopped off in bean fields. Cocklebur plants produce hundreds of little football-shaped burrs, about one inch long. They are covered with stiff, hooked spines that tend to stick to one's clothing. There is a story that a 3M scientist used the cocklebur as a model for the Velcro product.

In 1999, the largest flood in my memory occurred on the river. It followed a very heavy snowfall winter with a slow spring melt.

23

The entire state felt the effects of that spring melt, including the Red River and Mississippi basins. I was living in Plymouth, Minnesota, at the time and went to the farm with several friends to see the river. It was so high that we had to approach from a different direction than we usually do because of a flooded bridge over a creek. The flooded river was impressive. A normal flood might cover 1/4th of the lower field but this one covered more than half of the field. The normal two-mile-wide river basin was 1/3rd covered in water. It was one of the most amazing sights my friends and I had ever seen. The Mississippi had large floods that year through its entire length to the Gulf of Mexico.

# Chapter 7

# Fish and Fishing

The Minnesota River has a variety of fish species. Over the years I have fished most of them. In my early teens, my brother Truman and I used to take the tractor and trailer down by the river into the woods to our favorite walleye hole. We got minnows for bait from a local creek and used them for fishing walleyes. Even though we usually caught walleyes, other species liked our bait. We caught an occasional catfish, sucker, carp, and sometimes turtles. Mud turtles put up a good fight but it was the snapping turtles that fought hard while in the river and fought harder on land. Often we pulled out the 22 rifle and shot them to be able to retrieve our hooks. On one occasion we had a nice stringer of six walleyes in the water. We heard some commotion near the stringer and found a snapping turtle that had eaten five fish that looked like cartoon fish skeletons. The snapper was starting on the 6th when he got the 22-rifle treatment. We never had a good relationship with snapping turtles on the Minnesota River.

I caught my first large catfish with a good sized frog. I threw the bait into the fast-flowing center of the river. Not knowing what kind of fish would take the frog, I got a big hit on the line, set the hook, and started to reel in when the reel jammed and wouldn't turn. Assessing the situation, I turned and ran up the shore that was a wide sand bar. On the hook was a nice five-pound channel catfish.

We made many river trips over the years covering the distance from Granite Falls to 20 miles downriver from our farm. One of the first memorable fishing trips was with my cousins Phillip Rachie and James Finnes, a friend Carl Johnson, and myself. The trip started at the Echo bridge five miles upriver from our farm. Phillip and James shared a 12-foot boat with a small outboard motor. Carl and I shared my Herters 17 foot canoe. James and Phil could speed ahead because of their motor but would stop to fish, allowing us to catch up. Carl and I paddled and made good time even though we stopped to fish as well. At the end of the first day, we stopped downstream from the Belview bridge about four miles downriver from our farm. We camped on a sand bar and were up and on the river early in the morning. The second day we traveled slower, allowing me to get my view of the granite outcroppings that surfaced in that stretch of the river. There were some great fishing holes in that part of the river. We were most impressed by the beautiful outcroppings and how the river over time had shaped them. Late in the afternoon, Phillip's father, Uncle Oscar, met us at the Delhi bridge about 12 miles downriver from our farm. He had a large trailer that carried both our watercraft with ease. It was a great trip filled with adventure and sunburn.

River trips combined with camping out on a sand bar were a favorite activity of my sons and me. We had a Coleman 17-foot canoe that was very stable and cut through the water with ease. Using an old canvas tent we would camp on a sand bar and enjoy the beauty of the river and avoid mosquitoes. Large populations of bothersome black flies limited river activities in early June.

One memorable canoe trip included my two older sons, Jay and Jim, and our young Shih Tzu dog, Rueben. It was Rueben's first canoe ride, and as we went down the river he leaned on the side of the canoe looking at things going by. We weren't sure what he would do if we let him loose on the shore, but we stopped on a sand bar and let him out. Rueben raced up and down the sand bar and into the water. When he returned, he was wet, sandy, and exhausted. We took him home, bathed him, and he slept well that evening. One of his other great loves was riding in a milk crate on the back of my ATV enjoying the wind in his face.

Generally, our river trips used my 16-foot Aluma Craft Model K boat. My father and I bought it used in about 1965, and it spent most of its early life at our cabin on Scandinavian Lake. After we sold the cabin, I parked it at my Norwegian bachelor farmer Uncle Kenneth's farm close to the river. When we were planning a river trip, I would call Uncle Kenneth and ask how high was the river. He might reply, "Oh, it's kind of high," or "It's not too high." Though these answers gave me some information, I was glad when the DNR put up river level monitors both upriver and downriver. I often asked Uncle Kenneth to give us rides to take our vehicle from the starting point of our trips to the farm where we usually ended the trips. He was always willing to provide that service until one day when we asked him to do it. His reply was, "There are two of you; you should be able to work it out yourselves." It was then that we started to observe his mental decline with old age. He died at age 91 in 2001.

In the late 1990's my friend John Engel and I started to make trips downriver in the 16-foot boat, and catfish became the fish that we went after. We found catfish on the inside of a curve as the river went around a corner. Two to six pound catfish were very good eating. On one trip John and I rounded a bend and found that a pile of trees had completely blocked the river. We thought for a while, took off the boat motor, dragged the boat over the pile, and continued downriver. On that trip, we stopped at a sand bar and threw our bait out into the current catching nine channel cats. Their combined weight was under 30 pounds. Applying "The Engel Factor," John described the catch size as, "Going on 40 pounds!"

The early bait of choice was a stink bait called "Pole Cracker," manufactured by Catfish Charlies out of Oskaloosa, Iowa. It was our top choice for several years, and one time as I was driving through Iowa, I decided to visit Oskaloosa and lookup Charlie. Imagine my surprise as I asked for directions to Catfish Charlies only to learn that they had moved to another town.

We would bring along a cleaning board, frying pan, oil, stove, and Old Bay seasoning to prepare the fish. My friend Lowell Bonnema brought his son Ryan along on one trip. As we prepared the fish to eat, we served the fried fish on a foam plate. It melted through Ryan's plate and when he saw that, he was no longer hungry.

We found a new way to prepare catfish by using foil packets.

Spraying cooking oil on the foil to prevent sticking, we would place the filets on it and cover them with lemon slices. We added Old Bay Seasoning on top, and the foil packets baked over charcoal for 30 minutes. This is the recipe that we use to this day.

Uncle Jerry Peterson loved to fish for catfish on the Minnesota River. He was a fun-loving sportsman who also loved to hunt deer; more later on that. His son in law Nick Maki tells a story of one of his river fishing trips with Jerry.

"Jerry and I had lots of fun fishing and hunting together. We both enjoyed the friendly, good-natured back and forth banter as we would occasionally try to "One-Up" each other. I had taken Jerry fishing at my family's cabin on Sand Lake north of Virginia, Minnesota, where I grew up, and he reciprocated by taking me fishing on the Minnesota River. Jerry set me up in a good spot, and he went farther upstream and we started to fish. I wasn't having any luck so I decided to bring in my line and see if my bait was gone. I started to reel in when my line tightened up and I felt a little tug, so I leaned back and set my hook. I felt a couple of good thumps, so I kept my rod tip up and my line tight and the fight was on! I tightened the drag on my reel and was able to bring the line in, but the closer I got it in to shore, the harder the fish fought. Finally, I could see my hook and there was no fish on it, but there was some heavy fish line wrapped around it. I grabbed the line and could still feel the big fish pulling on it, so I thought all is not lost and started to hand line the big fish in. As I was doing this, I happened to look over to where Jerry was and I saw that he had a fish on his line also. It wasn't long before I realized that when he raised his rod tip to fight his fish, I felt a corresponding tug on the line I had in my hand. I figured his line must have wrapped around a log or rock in front of him and drifted downstream to where my line hooked it. Aha, here's my chance to have some fun with my father-in-law! As carefully as I could to keep him from seeing what I was up to if he looked in my direction, I started to give Jerry the fight of a lifetime! I would let him take in a little line and then I'd make a run that would strip the line off his reel and make it sing. After about ten minutes of this, I happened to see another fisherman sitting on a rock outcrop on the other side of the river. He was watching us, and it was obvious he knew what I was doing because he was laughing, waved at me, and gave me a thumbs up. Jerry happened to see the guy and turned to look in my direction. The jig was up, so I gave a couple of half-hearted tugs on the line that Jerry felt; I let go of his line and gave him a sheepish grin. The guy on the other side of the river stood up and applauded the performance. I thought I was going to have to walk home, but Jerry relented and let me back into his Bronco when we finished."

# Chapter 8

# Neighbors

Besides having many family members close to the farm, we had many great neighbors. Among those were men who rented the farmland until it entered the CREP program. Brothers Orlin and Elvin Sanders lived across the river and were experienced at farming within the river's flood plain. They loaned me a tractor and trailer to haul firewood after I cut down trees. They were also men of good character willing to help when needed. Alan Berends and his sons took over after the Sanders. They lived across the river next to our Howell Place farm. They farmed both farms with good farming practices. Also, being men of good character, they helped with other things as well as farming. Alan helped pull cedar logs from where we cut them to the Hilton where we could load them to the sawmill. He also helped with a couple of our Big Burns. When I had to cut large patches of Canadian thistles in the CREP acres, Alan loaned me his tractor and a large stalk chopper.

Dalen Caspers owns land near ours and we have had many interactions through the years. Dalen is a retired commercial artist who does pencil drawings, water color, and other mediums of buildings, scenes, and events. Dalen has done several drawings of our farm. The first one captured the barn and granary before they were gone. He next wanted to draw the log home but we had no photos of it so he asked me to sketch it. I did a computer rendering of the building and showed it to my mother. She made adjustments to the window size and height. Dalen knew the location of the home and we told him that there were hollyhocks in the front yard. With care he placed the drawing in the farm setting to record it for generations to come. My sons commissioned Dalen to draw, for my Christmas present, the machine shed that sits below the road. He did a great job capturing the scene, even adding a large buck and doe standing on the road. Whenever I go to the farm, I always call Dalen to catch up, since he doesn't have email or a smartphone for texts. I sometimes send him letters for things that need more explanation. We have had longs talks about land management, conservation, and character.

Lenny Holt owned the local locker plant in Sacred Heart. He also owned some wood lots near our farm, and we sometimes hunted deer together. Lenny and Julie had three sons who were great young men. The oldest trained in heavy equipment operation, the middle became a special education teacher, and the youngest is an electrician. I once asked Lenny how he raised such fine young men. He said that small-town social interactions centered around the church, school, and bars. He also added that he thought if the boys had a strong interest in the outdoors, fishing, and hunting that would be a good addition to school and church. Lenny contracted melanoma about ten years ago and put up a valiant fight but died four years later. His oldest son Mike helped in the locker plant during Lenny's last year and took over the business with his mother's help. Andy and Ryan also help when they can and own part of the business. Lenny started a tradition of butchering two deer for our hunting party for free. After his death, his sons continued the tradition for several years. We own adjoining wood lots near the river. We practice good communication and coordinating our hunting and fishing activities. The Holts are all good men of character. In the two sections below, Andy Holt shares two activities his family does in the river valley.

# Mushroom Hunting

The river valley offers many great opportunities for mushroom hunting. The low-lying, sheltered, moist areas in the valley offer everything needed for some interesting and tasty mushrooms to flourish. Some of the most common in our area include Morel, Chicken of the Woods, Oyster, and Pheasant Back. There are many others, but these are the ones most common that we find and enjoy. It is important to have a mushroom identification resource so you know what you are taking. A resource for great ways to prepare them to eat is a good idea as well. Mushroom hunting is a great way to connect with others and explore.

## Making Maple Syrup

The river valley offers a great opportunity for collecting maple sap to make maple syrup. The most common opportunity involves the Silver Maples that grow in the low-lying areas along the river. You may even be lucky enough to happen upon other forms of Maple. Silver Maple trees are great for syrup production. The sugar content of their sap is lower than that of a "Sugar Maple," but they are still a great option. You don't usually have to travel too far before you'll find an area where these trees are flourishing.

When the temperatures start climbing into the low 40's during the day, yet are still going below freezing at night, it is time to spring into action. You don't have forever, and this isn't something you can do whenever you want. That is part of what makes this such a wonderful experience. The tree is waking up for the year and the sap is the vehicle to get its spring processes started. When done correctly, this does not hurt the tree nor the habitat it grows in. After you have collected the sap and have enough to process, you boil it to remove the water. This takes a lot of boiling. You will likely need to boil off between 40 and 60 gallons of water for every gallon of finished syrup.

About 15 years ago, I decided that many of the trees on our woodlots were ready to harvest. I advertised, and a fellow from New Ulm answered, came to the farm to meet me, and had a look at the woods. He was interested in Basswood logs, of which there were many. We talked back and forth and finally agreed on a price per acre for the wood. He had an older pickup with a hunting knife stuck in the dash. I said to him that he seemed like a nice guy, but I didn't know him from Adam and he would have to pay for the wood before he started to cut. I went home and at the start of the next week, Lenny Holt called telling me that the guy had started cutting. I did not have his check, which presented a problem, so I called Renville County Sheriff Jerry Agre, who grew up next door to me, and asked what he could do. Jerry said he could do nothing "officially" but he would go down and talk to the guy. As the wood-cutter told me later, when he saw the Sheriff's car coming down toward him, he immediately stopped what he was doing.

He said the sheriff was nice enough, asking what he was doing and whose land he was on. He told me that he shut down his operation, went home, and sent the check to me. The Holts are men of good character.

Uncle Kenneth Homme was an interesting Norwegian bachelor farmer. He was the only millionaire in the family, but his wealth was in the form of farmland. He also raised purebred Angus cattle. He would keep a herd of about 40 cows and a couple of bulls. The bulls would breed the cows in the fall, and the next spring there would be a bunch of black calves. During the summer and into the fall, the cows and calves would graze on the pastures and hillsides of his farm. In the fall he would sell the calves to someone else to feed out for the market. This was a very profitable practice for him.

He bought the Kollen farm to keep it in the family and moved some of his cows there to graze. The state DNR did some analysis of the lands within the river valley. They found there to be a colony of endangered five-line skinks in the granite outcroppings on the farm. They offered to buy the land from Kenneth but didn't offer enough money. They tried several times to up their offer but he resisted. Kenneth asked me what I thought, and I suggested that he designate it as a wildlife area that would protect the skinks and preserve the land. The next year a sign went up declaring the land as the Homme-Kollen Wildlife Area.

With Indians living near the site at the end of the War of 1862, and having land that Indians once inhabited, Kenneth found many arrowheads, stone ax heads, and hammers. He had a good collection and asked me to build a display case for him. I made one out of birch plywood with a glass top and glass doors to display his finds. Upon his death, the collection was loaned to the Granite Falls Museum.

One adventure that my sons and I had with Kenneth was to pick wild plums. He loved wild plum sauce made by cooking plums, destoning, and adding a little sugar. To get the plums, we rode in the back of his pickup into the pasture. When we came to a plum tree, one of the boys would fetch a plum for Kenneth to sample. He would then declare the tree as acceptable or not. If acceptable we would spread out paint drop cloths under the tree and shake them to get the plums to fall. We then emptied them into a five-gallon bucket and moved to the next tree. Shortly, the pail was full enough and we brought it back to his sister, Aunt Guro. She prepared the sauce, which Kenneth then tasted and pronounced as great.

Grandson Jusitn Homme shows the history
of our cornbreeder Enestvedt cousins.

Pencil drawing of our log home by Dalen
Caspers. Used with permission.

The Homme Log Home
by Dalen Caspers
Limited Edition

Son Peter Homme monitoring "Big Burn # 1"

Grandson Jack lighting hillside during a
controlled burn. Ray Kunz in the background.

My good friend Dave Rodquist and me at
the mouth of Meadow Creek on the river.

John Homme, Jim Homme, and Dalen Caspers
sitting on the river bank

Late summer view of the bend of the Minnesota
River from what we call "The Best View.

John Homme cutting red cedar with Glenn
Huseby's Wood Mizer saw.

Martha Homme on the cedar chest I made for
our fortieth anniversary.

Good friend John Engel with a ten pound
flathead catfish caught on one of our river trips.

Jay Homme and Jim Homme posing for the
traditional Homme Hilton portrait.

Homme Hilton jackets
in varioius colors.

Granddaughter Savannah picking wild grapes
for jelly making.

Pencil drawing of Homme Hilton by Dalen
Caspers. Used with permission.

Ray Kunz, John Homme, and John Engel at the
2012 Big Red Rally.

John Homme cleaning a nice catfish
on the river bank.

Dave Rodquist, John Homme, Mike Lorentz, and
Ray Kunz with a 20-pound tom turkey.

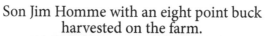

Son Jim Homme with an eight point buck
harvested on the farm.

An average size deer hunting crew of twelve.

Son Peter and granson Alexander overlooking
pelicans at the Granite Falls Dam.

# Chapter 9

# The Homme Hilton

This is how my good friend Mike Lorentz describes the Hilton:

"The wonder of the Minnesota River Valley at the HOMME HILTON. For about 14 years I have accompanied my friend to the farm he grew up on in the Minnesota River Valley south of Sacred Heart, Minnesota. My impressions today are that it is a beautiful place. That stretch of the river has native prairie grasses and undisturbed forest. I've seen birds that you don't find many places in Minnesota. It is a calming restful place to enjoy a quiet afternoon fishing or walking along the shore. For me, it's been a place of rest and renewal and reconnection with nature, with God, and with friends. I look forward to every visit and every time I find something new to wonder and enjoy."

Deer hunting has always been the social event of the fall in our family. We would stay with my parents in Sacred Heart, but when Dad died in 1983 and Mother moved in 1984 we needed to make other arrangements. For a couple of years, we stayed in my friend Arnold Petersen's comfortable motor home. The first year we learned that the furnace has its thermostat and battery to keep the place warm and the battery was dead. So someone had to get up periodically and start the engine to run the furnace. Arnold bought a new battery and the next night was warm. There were a couple of suitable buildings on the farm that we converted to

45

bunkhouses. My brother Truman and his group slept in an 8-foot by 12-foot building using a propane heater for warmth. I later converted a 10-foot X 17-foot building into a bunkhouse that would sleep ten, using a wood stove for heat. We named it The Homme Hilton.

It underwent several upgrades over the years. We added insulation, and after several years opened up an end wall to add six feet to the length of the Hilton, bringing its inside length to 17 feet. In doing so, we added enough bunk space to sleep 14. We then added a larger wood stove that I found on Craigslist for $50. The larger group size meant that we needed more space for cooking and eating. In the late 2000's we moved an 8-foot by 12-foot building to the end of the Hilton. We cut a doorway to the new kitchen dining area. With insulation, cabinets, and countertops, it became very functional. We say that the Hilton would be a five-star location but there is no valet parking. It has no running water either, but we have a generator and a bulb string like you'd see at a used car lot for lights. Having a place to stay on the farm has opened it up to many more activities. These include turkey hunting, fishing, berry picking, fellowship, and enjoying the beauty of the river valley.

In the 1990s there was a break-in at the Hilton that we didn't find out about right away. A Redwood County Deputy Sheriff stopped a car of adolescents across the river in Redwood County for erratic driving. When he approached the driver's window, the kid said, "The stuff in the trunk isn't mine." So the deputy said, "Open the trunk." In the trunk were camping and other items from the Homme Hilton, though the deputy didn't know that. When asked a further question, the kid told him where the items came from. He called the Renville County Sheriff's Department; Sheriff Jerry Agre said he knew to whom the items belonged. He called my brother, Truman, who called me. I went to the Hilton to check for damage and missing items. The judge asked what we wanted to do? I said that we would like $20 an hour for our time dealing with the situation. Also to tell the kids that if there was another break-in that their names would be at the top of the suspect list.

The Hilton has its clothing line consisting of caps, shirts, hats, and jackets. The caps are usually given to first-time Hilton guests. Each of my grandchildren get a Homme Hilton jacket their first sleepover in the Homme Hilton.

An activity that I started with my grandkids was making movies when we went to the Hilton. An early classic is CoCo Poo that explores the similar shape of CoCo Puffs cereal and deer poo. https://youtu.be/6yWd-j6dzCA See my granddaughters Katie, Natalie, Ashley, and me enjoying different activities and foods at the Hilton. Katie's classic line was, "I ate deer poo!" and Natalie's was, "EEE – EUU!"

Another Homme Hilton tradition is to have your special photo made on your first Hilton trip. The special photo is with a large set of deer antlers on your head and taken next to the Homme Hilton sign.

Sledding down the long and steep hill is another Hilton activity. The hill was once a road to the upper part of the farm; it was both exciting and scary. Lying down on runner sleds gave one a close view of what was ahead and added drama to the ride. The initial downslope was about 150 yards long with a 30-degree angle. Next comes a gentle right-angle turn at the bottom followed by a left angle turn to avoid the barn. If the track was good, the ride could cross the county road (with someone watching for cars). It could end about 200 yards in the lower field. Those rides were breathtaking and required courage to complete. My father, Peter, would leave his walking sticks next to the barn, and the grandkids would transform them into all sorts of imaginary things.

The barn on the farm had a log and wooden frame covered by corrugated metal. The roof consisted of boards covered by wood. The roof shingles rotted when water got to the underlying wood, causing the building to become unstable. We contracted with a local guy who had a backhoe that he used to bury the barn. The place it stood on is now the Hilton parking lot. There was also a granary, as mentioned before.

We pile garbage where the log home basement was and burn the garbage about every other winter. One of the burns was closer to spring, and when we left there was one smoldering piece of wood. I thought it would be no problem, but it flared up and burned over to the steel grain bin where we store things. The grass burned beyond the bin around the outhouse and stopped eight feet from the Hilton. The wooden base that the steel bin sat on burned and things inside the bin did also. Destroyed were a portable generator, tools, runner sleds, plywood & lumber.

Three runner sleds had the wood burned off of them and one had warped runners because of the heat. The other two runners were all right, so I decided to rebuild them. The first thing was to sand them clear and then paint them bright red. I used white oak from the farm to replace the wooden parts. The result were sleds that looked better than they had looked before.

One spring weekend, son Jay's kids were at the river exploring as kids will do. They set about trying to find out which parts of the muddy riverbank were dry enough to walk on and which weren't. They found both situations and in the process lost some shoes in the mud that Jay had to retrieve. Kids, water, and mud are a combination that is bound to spell adventure.

There was an old outhouse on the farm that needed replacing. I took measurements for materials to build one. But Cousin Steve Homme said that he had an extra outhouse at his cabin up north. So Steve and I borrowed a trailer and went to his cabin. The outhouse was well built of rough cedar and quite heavy. We put the trailer as close as we could, and using poles as levers, finally got the outhouse to lie down on the trailer. On the way home, we got lots of looks aimed at our cargo by fellow travelers. We took it to the farm the next day, dug a hole for it to stand upon, and dubbed it "The Hilton Head."

The Christmas before Martha and I got married, my father gave me a piece of log. He explained that I could have it and also take down the log home we had lived in for building materials. We planned to use these in the construction of the cabin we were building on Scandinavian Lake. We used Dad's tractor to pull the logs apart, salvaging the roof boards and other useable lumber. I planned to take the logs to a local sawmill and have them cut up for joist lumber. After a few test cuts, the sawyer told us there were too many nails in the logs and ruined the teeth in his blade. The log strategy then changed, and I advertised some logs for mantles. The rest we used for retaining walls at the cabin.

# Chapter 10

# Big Red Rally

One of the Hilton activities that has a life of its own is the Big Red Rally. In the early 1990's my friend Lowell Bonnema brought his Honda 180 cc 3-wheeler ATV to the Hilton. We used it to explore the farm and the surrounding area. It became very popular right away. My friend Ray Kuntz and I bought a 1985 Honda 250 Big Red 3-wheeler that we shared until 2000. Ray bought my half when we moved to North Carolina for six years. The Big Red had some issues that we repaired and it serviced us very well. Designed for farm work, the Big Red had very good pulling power to haul trailers and other heavy loads behind it. It also had 12-volt outlets for various tools. Another friend, John Engel, had a Honda 250 3-wheeler like the Big Red with fewer features. Disclaimer: Honda quit making 3-wheelers in 1987 because of safety issues about high-speed turnovers. We didn't run ours at high speeds but used them for their exceptional maneuverability.

After we moved back to Minnesota in 2006, I bought my own 1986 Honda 250 Big Red 3-wheeler. John Engel, Ray Kuntz, Lowell Bonnema, and I started The Big Red Rally. It consisted of several days of fellowship, ATV riding, fishing, and sight-seeing. The Rally grew over the years in participants, events, and reputation. John Engel tells a story in which he is the "rider and participant":

> "One participant, when stopping for gas, was asked about the annual Minnesota Midwest Regional Big Red Rally: where the rally was being held and how many participants attended? He shared that the rally lasted several days and attracted riders from all over the region. Af-

ter describing directions to the river and to the starting point, the rider then mentioned that he had placed third in last year's rally. Then he admitted and that he couldn't begin to estimate the total number of riders that attended every year, but that there was at least 5-6 registered in their little group. As he pulled away, he shouted, 'Hope to see you there!'"

We started to make movies about the Rally that only added to its legend. John Engel, who has a radio broadcast background, did most of the narration. One example is Big Red Rally 2012, September 11, 2012. https://youtu.be/Lxl0_9Ldo8Q That year's rally included three Honda Big Reds and two other red ATVs that qualified because of their color. There were cross-country events. That year's rally featured rifle, shotgun, and fishing events. We also had a potato cannon competition powered by cheap hairspray. That year's menu included a Friday night visit to the Grandview Valley Winery for pizza. Other meals included traditional grilled catfish from the river and an evening steak dinner grilled by Chef Ray.

On one Rally, we were sleeping in a screen tent on the river bank. While sitting around a fire we noticed some lightning in the southwest a ways away. Ray Kuntz had a radar app on his new iPhone and said there was rain near Marshall, about 50 miles away. So Ray set his watch to wake him every hour to recheck the rain's progress. He woke us about six a.m. and said we better head up to the Hilton. We quickly packed rain sensitive items and got to the Hilton as drops started to fall. By the time we got into our sleeping bags there was a downpour outside. We slept until nine.

The Rally has been the social event of the summer because it combines the elements that make the Minnesota River Valley so special. It has great views, terrain that has such variety, wildlife, plant varieties, and weather. Combine those elements together with friendship, fellowship, humor, ingenuity, explorations, and stories, and you have a great event.

Over the years the Big Red Rally changed and overlapped with the Fall Work Day, which was the Saturday after Labor Day. The rally would start on the previous Thursday. On Saturday, hunters came to prepare the Hilton for deer hunting. Tasks involved cutting firewood, stacking it in the Hilton, cleaning the Hilton, taking supply inventory, clearing shot lanes for hunting, mowing the parking area, fixing deer stands, and putting up "No Hunting" signs.

# Chapter 11

# DNR Catfish Species Workgroup

Because of my interest in the Minnesota River and its catfish population, I served on the Department of Natural Resources Catfish Species Workgroup starting on January 1, 2017, until December 31, 2018. The Workgroup fosters open communication, reviews technical information, and provides practical counsel to the DNR about the fishery. The workgroups hold no formal authority for policy or operations in the management of the fishery.

The workgroup has three meetings a year. The spring meeting is at the DNR headquarters in Hutchinson, Minnesota. It involves legislative updates, regulations, legislation, rules, education, fishing tournaments, public access, fish populations, and habitat work. The spring meeting also displays the DNR's equipment used for monitoring fish populations. The river biologists have jet-boats for operating in shallow water. One piece of sampling equipment includes an electrical shocking system that temporally stuns fish. They are collected, measured, categorized, and returned to the river. The electric shocking system has its limitations in that larger fish are usually deeper in the water. They are not affected by the shock and are excluded from sampling. Some fish are fitted with acoustic tags that aid in later growth and movement fish studies. At various locations on the river, there are electronic monitoring stations that record passing tagged fish. While sharing how the tagging worked, one of the river specialists told the story of a large tagged carp. It started by the mouth of the Minnesota River in St. Paul and two days later passed the monitoring station at Granite Falls, a trip of about 300 miles. One day later it was back at the mouth of the river again. This story illustrates that fish move up and down the river with ease. They don't congregate in one area for long periods. The exception to this is during the winter months when they find deep holes, slow their metabolism, and wait for warmer water.

A more effective method is using hoop nets that are about 4-feet wide and 20-feet long. Deployed for up to a day, they collect fish which are measured, categorized, and returned to the river.

The summer meetings are usually held on location and, in 2017 and 2018 they were held at the Homme Hilton. A short video illustrating the hoop net technique in Catfish Working Group Sampling, Aug 5, 2017. https://youtu.be/Fn3KHBsj_xU The fall meeting is usually a conference call covering most of the items covered in the spring meeting as well as updates.

I learned much about catfish in my workgroup tenure. There are three kinds of catfish in the Minnesota River, including the channel, blue, and flathead. Channel is the most prevalent, followed by blue. The flathead is the apex predator in the river, growing to large sizes (40 pounds is not uncommon, with a state record of 70 pounds) and old ages of up to 25 years. The flatheads are recent arrivals to the river; they are only located downriver from the Granite Falls Dam built in 1911. Turbines allowed the dam to provide electricity for the city of Granite Falls. When my Uncle Ole Homme returned from WWII, he was trained as an engineer. He went back to farming but took on extra work monitoring the workings of the turbines at the dam. Sometimes, when he was at work, my dad would take us to visit him at the dam. I remember his taking a rake and catching fish with it as they were trapped at the grate of the turbine inlet.

Above the dam are channel and blue cats. The flatheads are a prized trophy to a fisherman. Catfish fishing tournaments have sprung up on the Minnesota River. They provide prizes for the largest fish, usually a flathead. In years past the fish were brought to a weigh station to be registered. Later, large tanks were added at the weigh-in facility to display and keep the fish for their return to the river. Even with the tanks, the tournament flathead mortality numbers increased. It was through the efforts of the Catfish Working Group and other interested parties that photographic evidence of the catch is allowed for on-site catch and release. A smartphone application provides location and time data as well as recording the fish length relative to a measuring stick.

Gizzard Shad and Creek Chubs are a good bait to catch large catfish; worms and stink-bait work well for good eating sized fish. I remember seeing what my father called "Iowa Fishermen" come to the river with a can filled with a mixture of chicken blood and guts (internal organs). They usually headed home with their limits. Dad's hired man, Westly Benish, used set lines in the late 40's and early 50's for his catfish. They would consist of a long strong line with several hooks spaced at about 10-foot intervals with chicken internal organs as bait. He tied it to a secure log at the river's edge and waited a day or so to retrieve his catfish.

The working group also discussed invasive species that have made their way into the Minnesota River watershed. Among these are Asian carp imported from China in the 1970s to control plankton in aquaculture ponds. They have escaped from Southern states into open waters. The carp present a huge potential threat to the state's fisheries. They are voracious eaters with the ability to muscle out native fish.

Zebra mussels are small, fingernail-sized mussels that attach to solid surfaces in water. An Eastern European native, zebra mussels have been here for more than 20 years, and their presence causes more algae and weed growth and kills native clams.

The Catfish Working Group was an interesting and educational experience. In 2018 I resigned and suggested neighbor Andy Holt as my replacement. Andy is very river knowledgeable, younger, and very bright, making him a good asset to the Working Group.

# Chapter 12

# Deer Hunting

My cousin Phillip Rachie tells the story of how the white-tailed deer were reintroduced into the Minnesota River Valley in about 1947. It seems that early settlers killed off deer for meat and hides, so very few remained. Upriver in the Hawk Creek location, a farmer decided to raise white-tails in a fenced-in area. He was successful in breeding the deer but his fences were not high enough to keep them confined. Enough escaped, forming a breeding population for the river valley. Deer hunting seasons followed in the 1950s.

I went deer hunting with my brother and dad, and when I was 16 years old got a 16-gauge Mossberg bolt action shotgun. We could not use rifles for hunting in the valley. Shotguns used lead slugs instead of rifled bullets. During my first hunt on a snowy morning, we saw several deer running from left to right in front of us about 20 yards away. I fired three shots in their direction and saw the third slug hit a tree about 15 feet up, knocking some snow off. It was my first experience with "buck fever." The Mossberg had a bad habit of getting the slugs jammed in the clip, so I traded it for a 12-gauge Stevens 311 double barrel. It was with the double that I got my first deer at a distance of 60 yards, a very good shot with a slug. I used the double for several years, but it also had a defect that allowed me to set off both barrels at the same time, which caused considerable shoulder pain. It was then that I bought a 16-gauge Model 12 Winchester pump that I have to this day. It is a very reliable and accurate gun.

We continued to hunt as a family until my father died in 1983. After that my brother brought some of his friends. I brought some of mine and my sons. We had hunt rituals each year that included a deer count. Deer counts took place the Friday evening before the hunt and involved driving a prescribed route at sundown. We would count deer as an estimate of the population from year to year. In the 1980s and early 90s, these counts were never less than 50 deer and many times over 100.

The morning ritual of the hunt was to sit in stands waiting for deer to pass until about 9 a.m.. We then came in for coffee and shared stories. Being in the quiet woods while the sun rose was a wondrous experience. We would hear hunter shots, cows across the river, squirrels, turkeys, crows, and small birds. Overhead might fly a red-tailed hawk riding the thermals created by the hills. Because of the hills and ravines, sounds would play tricks on you. I wouldn't always know where the sounds were coming from and how far away the source was. When a deer came along it heightened the experience.

After a break for morning coffee and exchange of stories, the next ritual was to organize a drive. We posted shooters at one end of a wooded area and drivers walking from the other end of the area pushing deer toward the posters. The drive usually ended at about lunchtime. After lunch, we would go upriver to Uncle Kenneth's farm that covered most of a section. With his pickup, he would place the posters and tell the drivers to wait 15 minutes before starting to walk. His farm had a beautiful mixture of hillside, pasture, and field land that was prime deer habitat. It even had two natural springs that provided water for his cattle and the wildlife.

One hillside was filled with cedar trees, and when drivers walked through it they got quite a workout. He had one posting location that he called the "Sweet Spot" where he usually placed me or a new hunter. It was at the end of a natural funnel and I was certain to see deer coming right at me. I shot several deer in that spot. The drivers in the middle at Uncle Kenneth's farm had to walk through the hillside of cedars. I once took a chainsaw and attempted to cut a path through them. The chain jumped off track about halfway through and I gave up. Crawling through the cedars is a better way to describe what the drivers experienced than walking. They usually got some deer to come to the posters.

One year at Uncle Kenneth's we spotted a bunch of deer in his picked cornfield. One of the hunters volunteered to circle them and drive them back to the rest of the group. This was on a Sunday afternoon and we were looking for a buck to fill out one of our tags. Forty-one deer came at us from the field and split into two groups. Twenty-two went to the left past Lowell Bonnema and 29 came straight ahead toward us. We had to stand behind vehicles to avoid being trampled. We were looking for horns and didn't see any. What a beautiful sight to see that many animals up close.

During the 1980's we had the pleasure of hosting Uncle Jerry Peterson from Redwood Falls and his son cousin Les. They were both passionate hunters and usually sat on the upper west side of the farm. They continued to be part of the hunting party until the early 90s when they both passed on.

In 1982 Steve Homme moved into the house across the street from us in Plymouth. I didn't know Steve, but when he saw our name on the mailbox, he came across and introduced himself. We compared family and found that his great grandfather and my grandfather were brothers. Steve usually hunted deer in northern Minnesota with two friends. After a week of hunting, the three would come home with two deer to share. My father thought it would be a good idea to invite Steve to hunt with us in the Minnesota River Valley. Steve accepted and bought a new 12-gauge shotgun with a scope on it. On the first morning of the 1983 season, I put him in a stand that I thought would provide some action for him. Shortly after 8 a.m. I heard four shots and went over and asked Steve, "Did you get one?" He replied, "I think I got two, I shot one down over here, It got up and I shot it down again. Then I shot another one down over there and it got up and I shot it down again." When we went to inspect, we found that Steve had gotten four deer with four shots. We dressed the deer and took them down to the barn and took a picture. It was time for the morning drive by then, and we told Steve to take off his scope because he was a driver for the rest of the day. During the start of the next drive, a nice 8-point buck circled back through the drivers. Steve dropped to one knee and had deer number five. He took a lot of ribbing during lunch. Uncle Kenneth was waiting for us at about 1 p.m., setting the posters and taking the drivers to the starting point. While on the way there, Kenneth spotted a deer in the field, stopped the pickup, and pointed. Steve shot deer number six. When the drive started, a deer popped up in front of Steve and he bagged number seven. We had 17 hunters that year and we filled all 17 tags on the first day of hunting. Steve took a lot of ribbing from the group and when he got to work on Monday his coworkers called him a flat-out liar. It was before digital cameras were invented. He had to wait until Wednesday to get the developed photos and prove his story. The following season we asked Steve how he was going to top last year. He only got one deer in 1984, but it was a huge buck that made it to the Minnesota Deer Classic. (The Classic requires an antler total measurement of at least 150 inches; Steve's was 156 inches.)

One deer story (shared on the promise of anonymity) was one of our hunters coming back to the "Hilton" at dusk. He said he saw a deer that could have passed as an elk. (A large elk would have bragging rights over a deer.) It was a once in a lifetime deer! But he couldn't get a shot off. Racked with guilt, years later he fessed up and said he had a perfect shot at this once -in- ten lifetime's deer. It was an easy shot—couldn't have missed even if blindfolded. His only mistake was that he forgot to load the gun.

One season as we finished a drive, we followed a wounded doe to the river. She started across with several of the hunters firing at her. She was finally hit on the far shore and fell dead. There was considerable discussion about how the deer would be retrieved. Finally, son Jay volunteered to wade the river and get it. He rolled up his pants and started across. The river was low and he only got wet up to his thighs. He put a rope around the deer's neck and pulled it back. I asked him if he could recreate the event because I didn't have my camera. He declined.

In 1991 son Jay posted in a large snowy ravine behind the Hilton. A large buck came by; he shot and followed it a short distance where he did a killing shot. Lowell heard the shot and went to help dress out the buck. There were two ways presented to get it back to the Hilton—either down the treacherous ravine or up the side of the ravine that was 100 yards at a 45-degree angle. Three of the hunters pulled the buck up the hill and down to the Hilton. It was a very nice buck measuring about 145 inches of horn.

Almost 30 years later, Jay's son Justin was sitting in a ravine when a large buck came by him that he shot and killed. He had a cell phone and texted his dad for help get it out. His Uncle Jim was closer and helped dress the deer and pull it out. The two of them said the hill was very high and was hard to climb, but they got it home. It had a head that was worthy of being mounted. My advice/question to Justin was, "Next time could you shoot them closer to the road?"

Dave Rodquist has been a close friend for 30 years and has hunted with us for about 15 years. He earned the nickname of "One-Shot Dave" because when he shot at a deer it took only one shot to kill it. This went on for several years until he saw a very large buck walking by him about 20 yards away. He could tell it was wounded by the way it walked. He held off shooting as it came to the top of a deep ravine where it started down, tripped, and rolled to the bottom. It appeared to be dead. He asked for help, I came with an ATV and 75 feet of rope. Others went down and dressed out the huge animal. As they attempted to pull the buck up the ravine, it was plain that it would be a monumental task. They got it far enough up that we were able to tie the rope to it. I pulled it up about 20 feet at a time as that was all the space available. We would then back up, reattach the rope, and pull again. It took three repetitions of this process to get this monster to the top. We hauled it out on the front of the ATV, and Dave's new nickname became "No Shot Dave."

Since the early 1980s, we have kept a deer hunting logbook for each season. Records include the date, the weather, and a list of hunters. To this basic information we added any stories that the recorder would like to tell. The stories are filled with adjectives like good, great, huge, small, cold, warm, wet, and dark. These usually precede nouns such as food, weather, shot, drive, fellowship, weather, and morning. Over the years there have been wonderful stories that the log helps us to remember.

Awards and prizes are often given in relation to the hunt. A traveling trophy of a Bambi doll is given to the hunter who gets the smallest deer. Homme Hilton hats and caps are often rewarded by some form of drawing. In the 1990s my mother made some of her famous rice pudding for our Saturday evening desert. The hunters loved it, and I had to learn the recipe and have made it since her passing. She was a master quilter and made over 150 teddy bears as well. She would make one for a door prize for each hunt, and they were prized by the winners.

Over the years our hunting party has added new members and said goodbye to others. A few years ago I asked the group what they liked best about deer hunting. No one said "killing deer" was their favorite part. Fellowship, being outdoors, the beauty of the setting, and working together were high on their lists of favorites.

# Chapter 13

# Duck Hunting

Ducks would follow the river on their annual migration south. Hunting them on the river was a challenge because we had no boat or dog to retrieve downed birds. Pass shooting was a strategy we adopted that involved shooting the ducks flying over the land. Pass shooting had limited success for us. On Thanksgiving Day 1958, Uncle Jerry said that there was a large flock of Mallards sitting on an open section of the river. With some organization, Dad, Cousin Phillip, Jerry, and his dog, sneaked up on the flock. We could hear them well before we saw them as they were quacking to one another. It was a pristine morning, with freshly fallen snow on the ground and frost on the trees. As we neared the ducks, we spread out and agreed that Jerry would fire the first shot. When he did, the flock took off in one of the most beautiful sights I have ever seen. We knocked down about a half dozen, some of them falling in the river. Jerry tried to get his dog to jump in after the downed ducks. He even threw shotgun shells in the water to entice the dog. The dog would have no part of the cold water, and several of the ducks floated downriver under the ice.

# Chapter 14

# Turkey Hunting

In about 1962, Uncle Kenneth and Cousin Phillip bought several dozen wild turkey chicks. They planned to raise them and release them into the wild to start a hunting population. Bird science would find out later that the first moving creature the chicks saw would be imprinted on them as their parent. The chicks grew into large birds and were very friendly to humans. I remember driving in the river valley about 10 miles down-river from Uncle Kenneth's. There was a flock of turkeys on the road. I stopped, they came to the car window and we gobbled back and forth for a while after which I slowly drove away. A year or so later the flock was shot and killed. It was a sad ending to an interesting experiment.

In the late 1980s, the DNR brought two strains of wild turkeys from Missouri into the river valley. Normal wild turkeys have very good hearing and eyesight. They can run 30 mph and fly 50 mph and will flee at the first sign of trouble. We spotted birds from time to time and eventually there were enough to have a hunting season. It was during one of these early seasons that Cousin Steve and I tried our luck. Steve was set up in the woods with a turkey decoy and a call. Using a hen call, he got the attention of a tom turkey that came toward him gobbling as he came. Steve called enough to keep him coming. When the gobbling became louder, indicating it was close, Steve took the safety off his gun. Just then a bald eagle swooped down and grasped the decoy. Realizing it wasn't a real turkey, the eagle flew away and the tom turkey also lost interest. The only evidence of the encounter were the talon marks on the decoy.

Our neighbor Dalen Caspers is an avid bow hunter and turkey

hunter. He is very adept at calling in tom turkeys and does so for his sons and grandsons. We have asked him, over the years, for tips on his techniques. He told us he uses a slate call and tries to make a purring sound to call the toms in. We tried the purr for several years without much success and finally asked Dalen to come for a lesson. We were doing the purr right but were not getting the tom's attention first. He told us to use a loud box call to get their attention followed up by purring every 15 minutes. That morning I went to my stand by 8:30 a.m. and used the box call followed by purring. At 9:15, two toms walked by about 60 yards out and it didn't look as if they were coming closer. I shot at the larger one and landed my first 20-pound turkey. Hunting partner Dave Rod-quist showed me how to dress the bird. We made a fan of the tail and the beard that now hangs on my basement wall. The turkey breasts were delicious when fried in butter.

# Chapter 15

# Squirrels, Crows, Gophers, Groundhogs, Foxes, and Yotes

This category includes species that I have hunted or had interactions with over the years. They were classified as varmints at one time. These are pests or nuisance animals that spread diseases or destroy crops or livestock. There were large populations of squirrels on the farm especially when our corn cribs were full of corn cobs. The practice was to let the corn dry out over the winter in the cribs and shell the corn in the spring. Today most corn is harvested with higher moisture content and dried on the farm or at the elevator, thus skipping the shelling step. My brother and I had 22 rifles that we used to shoot squirrels in the corn cribs. Big yellow squirrels or small red ones were the two species that we hunted on the cribs and surrounding trees. The squirrels were very quick. They would run up a tree, jump across to another branch, and continue down that tree or into a hole in the trunk. With my semiautomatic 22, I would shoot at them while they ran and often found it was a waste of ammunition. When I wasted too many shells, I would switch to my single shot 22 that made me aim better and take good shots. I even picked one-off as it jumped between trees in the air. Squirrels had a habit of hiding behind the trunk of a tree. Knowing that there was one behind the trunk, I would walk up to the tree and then move around the base until the squirrel came into view, and the rest was history for the squirrel.

I once found a baby squirrel that had fallen out of a tree and kept it as a pet. It was very friendly and often sat on my shoulder. Its favorite sleeping place was in my dad's cap that hung in the back hall. He would climb up the clothing hanging there and get inside the cap. You wouldn't know he was there unless you knew where to look. The squirrel had a habit of hiding food (which squirrels do) in Mother's furniture. She would find stashes and other things and finally declared the squirrel had to go. I released him to the back yard, We saw him for a few days and then he disappeared. It was a fun experience.

Crows are very crafty birds hunted by several means to control their numbers. Some hunters use loudspeaker systems, sounding a crow's feeding call that would draw many crows to the hunters. I have been on a couple of these hunts, and they are very exciting and noisy. The crows flying by were an easy target for a shotgun. When I was driving the tractor doing fieldwork, I would often bring my 22 rifle along to shoot varmints. Crows were a hard target because as soon as the tractor stopped they would fly away. One time I was dragging a field that had a neck (a part of the field with some trees hiding it from the main part of the field) that came out in it. I spotted a crow on the field and went past the neck and stopped the tractor but left the motor running at regular speed. I then crept through the neck and shot the crow at about 30 yards distance.

There are two kinds of gophers in the river valley—the pocket and striped. The striped is the model for the University of Minnesota mascot. Striped gophers are curious in that they are often seen standing upright next to their holes. At the first sign of trouble, they will disappear down the hole to safety. If a hawk or fox finds them away from their hole, they are likely to be on its menu. I used to hunt striped gophers as a varmint with my 22. When we plowed the field, we would often cover a gopher's hole and they would scramble to find shelter. I once caught a baby and kept it as a pet for a while. Pocket gophers can be identified by the dirt mounds that they make when clearing underground for their boroughs. These mounds are generally found in groups that indicate a group of pocket gophers together. The county put a bounty on them at one time, and I trapped some by digging down to a borough and setting a trap. I rarely saw one outside its hole.

Groundhogs could be a major nuisance by digging under

buildings or in open fields. These creatures could reach 25 pounds in size and had nasty dispositions. We have filled and blocked their access under buildings. I once came upon a 20-pounder next to his hole in the field where I was turning hay with a fork. He hissed at me, and I dispatched him with the four-tine fork.

Foxes and yotes (coyotes) compete for the same small mammal food sources. Until the early 1980s, foxes were without competition from coyotes. Then the yotes moved in from the west and forced the foxes out. In high school, one of our favorite Sunday afternoon activities was to do a fox hunt at Uncle Kenneth's farm. Some of the guys carried shotguns and some 22 rifles. Uncle Kenneth had a varmint rifle, a K222, which sighted in at 400 yards and had a muzzle velocity of over 3000 feet per second. The shotgun carriers were drivers pushing foxes to the guys with 22's and Uncle Kenneth sat on the crest of a hill with his K222 watching for any long shots. We didn't always get a fox but had a good time in the outdoors with friends. Uncle Kenneth once found a baby fox and kept it as a pet for a couple of years.

Coyotes moved in from the Dakotas. We would see them from time to time but my first up-close experience was sitting in a deer stand with Scott Shetler. Scott sat facing me and was to alert me if any deer were coming from behind me. His eyes got big. I whispered, "Is it a buck?" He pointed to my right, so I switched my gun to prepare for a left-handed shot as a coyote came into view. One-shot to his shoulder sent him to his grave. I took the carcass to a man in town who skinned it and sent it off for tanning. The hide hangs in my son Peter's three-season porch next to a wolf skin from Mongolia (that's another story).

My neighbors, the Holt brothers, take yote hunting to a higher level. They own a locker plant and have plenty of leftover meat scraps to attract yotes. At first, they used leg traps but later switched to cable snares. The snares consisted of a cable in a loop deployed across a path where yotes run. The yote would catch itself in the loop and choke itself to death. Early snares sometimes caught deer. They were modified with a release that triggered at about 50 pounds, releasing any animal larger than that. Andy Holt and his brothers average taking about 10 yotes off our land and their woodlots each year. They have other snare areas as well and might get 35 yotes in a winter. The carcasses with hides sell for $20-$30 each.

# Chapter 16

## Hawks, Eagles, Turkey Vultures, Whip-poor-wills, and Pelicans

These beautiful birds are found in the river valley, some all year long, except the vultures only make seasonal appearances. We do not hunt these birds but love to observe them hunting for food and flying by. Red-tailed hawks are prevalent all year long in the valley. They float riding the thermal updrafts caused by the hillsides, always watching the ground for their favorite small mammals or snakes. They have excellent eyesight and it is fun to watch them dive at high speed to catch unsuspecting prey. They will usually take their meal to a tall tree and eat it there.

Bald eagles hunt like hawks but their main diet consists of fish. I have found some large nests near the river that they make to rear their young. They are the apex predator of the birds. Blackbirds will harass them by flying above them and pecking them. Because of their large size, the eagles have little defense against the smaller blackbirds. I have seen them sitting in a tall tree next to the river watching the current go by. Suddenly they will drop into a steep dive to catch a fish in their sharp talons. They sometimes overestimate their ability to fly away with a large fish, and have to let go because they are not very good swimmers. It's a great sight to see bald eagles flying up the Minnesota River.

Turkey Vultures are about the size of a small wild turkey. They have an ugly head and are always searching for animals, living or dead, to feast upon. Once I observed several of them overhead looking down at us. I finally realized that they were interested in our 12-pound Shih Tzu, Ruben. We put Ruben out of sight and they lost interest. Each spring for several years, I've seen turkey vultures sitting on our metal machine shed. One day as I was getting some sawed lumber from the shed, I heard some hissing. The sound was coming from under the woodpile, and as I looked under it, I found two turkey vulture chicks. We named them Orville and Wilber. Eventually, their mother taught them how to fly and hunt for themselves. The same female came back for several years to repeat the birth and rearing cycle in the same spot.

Whip-poor-wills are medium-sized birds. They have a large, rounded head and a stout chest that tapers to a long tail and wings. Named after its song, we hear Whip-poor-wills often after sundown at the farm. Some quiet evenings, their song will keep me awake. I have taken a bright flashlight to find them and try to scare them away to interrupt someone else's sleep.

We often see white pelicans going after fish in the river. One of their hunting techniques is to swim in a line driving fish ahead of them until they surface, at which time they snap them up. We have gone to the Granite Falls Dam several times to see 100 plus pelicans sitting on rocks or swimming around to catch fish. They must be successful because there are so many of them.

# Chapter 17

## Moose, Black Bear, Cougar, Elk, and Sasquatch

Though they are not native to the Minnesota River Valley, some large mammals pass through and are noticed by the folks living there. On our farm, there was a cougar sighting a few years ago. Downriver, moose and black bear have been sighted and photographed. Across the river, an elk was sighted last fall. We are still waiting for Bigfoot to put in an appearance.

# Chapter 18

# All Wet

This section may imply that my life is centered around water, which is not the case. I believe that growing up next to the Minnesota River had a major effect on my interests. The river gave me comfort, understanding, appreciation, and love for it and all things connected to it. When someone asks me where I am from, I reply Sacred Heart, but the picture in my mind is our farm on the Minnesota River. Many of my water adventures have taken place away from the river but tie back to my early experiences there.

In chronological order, my other adventures include building a sailboat. It was only 10 feet long with a single sail, but I learned the basics on it. We sailed on several lakes, including Green Lake, which was about 40 miles from the farm and was a favorite place. Martha reminds me that I took her sailing on our second date and turned the boat over. I remind her that she looked really good wet.

In my early teaching years, two of my students and I did a water study on Twin Lake in Robbinsdale, Minnesota. We tested five nutrients in the water. The main outcome of our tests verified that the salt used to melt road ice followed the storm sewers into the lake. Because of building Brookdale Shopping Center, Shingle Creek was rerouted away from Twin Lake. That left it with many inlets but no outlet. The effect was that it became a "dead sea" with nutrients building up in it. Our study confirmed that the chloride (salt) content rose from 2.6 parts per million (ppm) in 1952 to 120 ppm in 1970. Our work resulted in The Sun Newspaper naming me "The Man of the Year in the Environment." Testing in subsequent years confirmed the salt level has continued to rise.

We built a cabin on Scandinavian Lake in 1970. My cousin

Wilson and I, along with our wives Polly and Martha, took on the project. We found a house in Wilmar that needed to be moved and bought it for $100. Will and I then built a cement block foundation and capped it. A house mover charged us $550 to move the house 40 miles and place it on our basement. From there, we added a room, plumbing, insulation, electric heat, and a well. We owned the cabin for 20 years and enjoyed it with our growing family.

During that time I decided to build another sailboat. This one was a catamaran that had two hulls and rudders and a sail that I sewed myself from Dacron. It was a very fast boat that was quiet as it cut through the water.

In 1991 we sold the lake cabin because our co-owners moved out of Minnesota. In the 1990s, Martha and I vacationed every summer on Ocracoke Island, part of the Outer Banks of North Carolina . It was the base of operations for Blackbeard (Edmund Teach) from 1816-1818. Blackbeard's main method of operation was to wait for ships to run aground in the island's sandbars. He then sent his men to remove any valuable cargo. He often resold the cargo to the company that owned the shipwrecked ship. The army sent a ship in 1818 to put an end to Teach's enterprise. We enjoyed the ocean, beach, deep-sea fishing, history, and the locals of Ocracoke.

I have had several chances to fish in Canadian waters. First with my brother Truman, then with friend Terry Zuehlke, and then five other men from church. The church fly-in was a special adventure in that we drove to the Canadian border and then drove eight hours northeast to overnight at a motel. The next morning we flew northeast for an hour and landed on Lake Saganaga where we stayed in a newly built log house. We had access to three boats with motors and paired off for fishing. We fished with a new man each day. Walleyes and Northern Pike were the main species in the lake. I estimated that we caught between 400 and 500 fish that week. Catching fish became so common that I would often pull the lure aside if "only" a five pound Northern was chasing it. I only wanted bigger ones. The largest Northern caught by our group was about 45 inches and I caught the largest Walleye at 28 inches.

In 2000 we moved to Pinehurst, North Carolina, to take care of Martha's aging parents. A couple of years later we bought a beach condo at North Myrtle Beach. It was a great place to spend time with family and friends. By 2006 both of Martha's parents had passed away, and we were getting more grandchildren in Minnesota. We sold the beach condo for 2 ½ times what we paid for it and bought a home on Dutch Lake in Howard Lake, Minnesota. We sold our Pinehurst home and bought a golf condo so we could return in the winters. Our plan for life on the lake included fishing, tubing, and having grandkids come to visit. That plan worked well for a couple of years, but the grankids got busy and it was harder to carve out periods for them to visit. So in 2010, we decided to move to Rochester where most of our grandkids were living. Our two oldest sons are physicians at Mayo Medical Clinic. Our youngest son is an engineer with T-Mobile in Minneapolis. We bought a bank home, fixed it up to our liking, and got involved with the local community.

After the major Zumbro River flood in 2010, I became involved with the recovery effort with an organization called Zumbro and Friends. Its main effort was to connect people with recovery needs with people who had resources to help. Zumbro and Friends worked with the engineering department at University of Minnesota Mankato. Together they developed a water flow model of the Zumbro River Watershed. The model will help in predicting future floods and the help flood mitigation projects might have on preventing floods.

In one of our North Carolina winter visits, we went back to North Myrtle Beach. We bought another beach condo that we enjoy along with family and friends. We offer it for rent through Vacation Rental By Owner (VRBO) to help cover expenses.

To summarize, my family introduced me to the Minnesota River and my wife Martha introduced me to the ocean.

John Homme

# Acknowledgments

To God who has allowed me to have so many experiences involving water in my life. To my wife, Martha Homme, who did the initial editing and encouraged me. To Wilson Anderson, Dave Ogren, Pat Day, and Ray Kuntz who were my readers and secondary editors who saw things to add or explain. To my father, Peter Homme, and mother, Lena Homme, who instilled in me a love of the river valley. To my sons, Jay, Jim, and Peter, and grandchildren who helped me see the valley from a new perspective. To Dave Rodquist, Mike Lorentz, Andy Holt, and Nick Maki who added stories of their river valley experiences. To all the neighbors and friends who have enhanced my Minnesota River experiences over the years.

CPSIA information can be obtained
at www.ICGtesting.com
Printed in the USA
LVHW020030010721
691512LV00006B/139